What Tree are you eating from?

Dr. Apostle Rose

Giving all glory and honor to our Lord and savior

This short teaching is to help us think as well as meditate on the Word of God

Different versions of the Holy Scriptures are used

NKJV, EVS, and NIV

Always use different versions to help you understand what you are reading along with the

Holy Spirit

@ALRM 2023

Foreword

I was just meditating on the Word one day and the Holy Spirit put this in my heart to write down. What Tree are you eating from? I pray this study booklet helps you to decide on the tree you prefer to eat from. The Word of God tells us in Gospel Luke 6:44-49 NIV 44 Each tree is recognized by its own fruit. People do not pick figs from thorn bushes, or grapes from briers. 45 A good man brings good things out of the good stored up in his heart, and an evil man brings evil things out of the evil stored up in his heart. For the mouth speaks what the heart is full of.

Some say a lot of things, but their actions prove it every time out of the heart: Matthew 15:18 But the things that come out of a person's mouth come from the heart, and these defile them. 19 For out of the heart come evil thoughts—murder, adultery, sexual immorality, theft, false testimony, slander.

I Pray this booklet will be helpful to you in your studies of the Word.

Table of Content

Notes

What tree are you eating from, or should I say what fruits are you producing?

One day as I was meditating to minister the word, I began to think of Adam and Eve in the garden. You know where the story begins to speak of them and their existence. We know the story but let me just inject the scriptures here from the KJV and for simple reading the NIV texts. Genesis 1:26-31 KJV) *And God said, let us make man in our image, after our likeness: and let them have dominion over the fish of the sea, and over the fowl of the air, and over the cattle, and over all the earth, and over every creeping thing that crept upon the earth. 27So God created man in his own image, in the image of God created he him; male and female created he them. 28 And God blessed them, and God said unto them, be fruitful, and multiply, and replenish the earth, and subdue it: and have dominion over the fish of the sea, and over the fowl of the air, and over every living thing that moves upon the earth. 29 And God said, Behold, I have given you every herb bearing seed, which is upon the face of all the earth, and every tree, in the which is the fruit of a tree yielding seed; to you it shall be for meat. 30 And to every beast of the earth, and to every fowl of the air, and to everything that crept upon the earth, wherein there is life, I have given every green herb for meat: and it was so. 31 And God saw everything that he had made, and behold, it was very good. And the evening and the morning were the sixth day.*

NIV Genesis 1:26-31 26 Then God said, "Let us make mankind in our image, in our likeness, so that they may rule over the fish in the sea and the birds in the sky, over the livestock and all the wild animals, and over all the creatures that move along the ground." 27So God created mankind in his own image, in the image of God he created them; male and female he created them. 28God blessed them and said to them, "Be fruitful and increase in number; fill the earth and subdue it. Rule over the fish in the sea and the birds in the sky and over every living creature that moves on the ground." 29Then God said, "I give you every seed-bearing plant on the face of the whole earth and every tree that has fruit with seed in it. They will be yours for food 30 And to all the beasts of the earth and all the birds in the sky and all the creatures that move along the ground-everything that has the breath of life in it-I give every green plant for food." And it was so. 31God saw all that he had made, and it was very good. And there was evening, and there was morning-the sixth day

*A*fter God (ELOHIM) completed all the earthly creation and filled it with the animals, fowls, reptiles etc.… He decides to make man and let him oversee the beautiful creation he made. God deem humanity worthy to oversee his marvelous work. That makes me feel a little special. The creator made us in his image and in his likeness. I do believe some of his likeness is love, trust and giving. Just naming a few right off the top. You know what is a part of our Creator? Unity. Why do I say that? God did nothing without the son and the Holy spirit. They agreed when they made man as well as established the redemption plan for humanity.

See how good our Father is. He told them what to do and then he said, "I give unto you. Give you means it's yours. Genesis 1:*29 Then God said, "I give you every seed-bearing plant on the face of the whole earth and every tree that has fruit with seed in it.*

God the Father gave people every seed-bearing plant on the face of the earth for food. Man didn't have to worry about food. If he supplied their food, do you not think that the shelter was supplied as well? Just think about the God that we serve. Matthew 6:33 tells us Matthew 6:33 KJV [33] But seek ye first the kingdom of God, and his righteousness; and all these things shall be added unto you. What shall be added just read the verses before this one, which plainly tells us if he makes a way for the fowls and the flowers what about you and me. Shelter, food, water, and clothing will be provided. Hallelujah. We must understand this, God places people in your life or just passersby to be a blessing to you. Everything shall be provided because the Word declares the earth is the Lords. (Psalm 24:1) Psalm 24:1 The earth is the Lord's, and the fulness thereof; the world, and they that dwell therein. Deuteronomy 10:14 Behold, to the Lord your God belong heaven and the highest heavens, the earth and all that is in it. 1 Chronicles 29:11 Yours, O Lord, is the greatness, the power, the glory, the victory, and the majesty, indeed everything that is in the heavens and the earth; Yours is the dominion, O Lord, and You exalt Yourself as head overall. These are just a few scriptures to let you know that God is the creator and yes, he is the head and owns everything. He can raise up or tear down. He is the potter, and we are the clay.

Take a few minutes and search for more scriptures to back up what has already been said. Sometimes we as teachers of Word most seek out a few more references from the Word to help our listeners to understand this. God is our maker. We are not the maker but the works of his mighty hands.

Now back to the Garden: in the garden God gave humanity a choice and command. It was on them whether they chose to obey or not. Just like it is today. We have a choice in this life to eat from the tree of life or eat from the tree of good and evil. My question is "Which tree are you eating from?"

Notes

Choice and decision: To Obey and Live or Disobey and die

I label this topic to obey and live or disobey and die simply because this is the choice God gives us all. And this started in the Garden.

When we read about creation and then the fall of man believe this it did not all happen over a brief period of time. Adam was present with every fowl, beast, reptile, fish, etc. and he named each one that was brought before him. I am quite sure that this took him time to do.

Let me just insert these passages of scriptures. Genesis 2:8-15 [8] Now the LORD God had planted a garden in the east, in Eden; and there he put the man he had formed. [9] The LORD God made all kinds of trees grow out of the ground-trees that were pleasing to the eye and good for food. In the middle of the garden were the tree of life and the tree of the knowledge of good and evil. [10] A river watering the garden flowed from Eden; from there it was separated into four headwaters. [11] The name of the first is the Pishon; it winds through the entire land of Havilah, where there is gold. [12] (The gold of that land is good; aromatic resin and onyx are also there.) [13] The name of the second river is the Gihon; it winds through the entire land of Cush. [14] The name of the third river is the Tigris; it runs along the east side of Ashur. And the fourth river is the Euphrates. [15] The LORD God took the man and put him in the Garden of Eden to work it and take care of it.

Now from reading these passages of scriptures. God created heaven and earth and all there in and he made man in his image. Chapter 1 says male and female. We get to chapter 2 a remake of 1 but added information so we can see a better picture.

So, after God made everything, he decided to pick out a place for humanity, the garden of Eden. In this garden everything man needed was there. Also, in this chapter we are introduced to the **tree of life** and **the tree of knowledge of good and evil**. Now did you notice this? It said in the center of the garden were these trees. The center of attention which Adam truly didn't have time to investigate since he was given the task of naming all the beasts, fowls, reptiles, and whatever else God had for him to name. You know when we are focused on the word of God, praying in seeking his face, we do not have time to be bothered with other things that are not feasible to us. It's those times when we take our eyes off Jesus is when we begin to make the wrong choices and decisions. God even told Adam what was good for him to eat. Every seed-bearing tree that also was pleasing to the eyes.

Think for a minute, how many times have we taken our eyes off the word and begun to dab in the flesh and ended up making the wrong decision? How often do we pray to give us our daily bread but will not digest what is given us in the word? What gets us is our flesh and desiring to know is what gets us in trouble.

God gave them the trees with the fruit that was pleasing to the eyes but still the eye wandered off. Question: how did the eyes begin to wander? Of this, chapter 2 of Genesis tells us that Adam looked around and God said, man should not be alone. So, he took out time and fashioned a woman from the rib of a man. Not the back side but the rib. The rib, the protective covering of our major organs in our bodies.

In the Garden, Genesis 2:15-18 [15 The] LORD God took the man and put him in the Garden of Eden to work it and take care of it. [16 And] the LORD God commanded the man, "You are free to eat from any tree in the garden; [17 but] you must not eat from the tree of the knowledge of good and evil, for when you eat from it you will certainly die." [18 The] LORD God said, "It is not good for the man to be alone. I will make a helper suitable for him."

Right here are these passages of scriptures. He told man to work and take care of the garden, then he commanded man "you are free to eat from any tree in the garden, but you must not eat from the tree of knowledge of good and evil. Please note that he didn't tell them they couldn't eat of the tree of life. This let me know one thing, in life the very thing we should not do is what we find ourselves doing. Apostle Paul said this; Roman 7:15-25 15 I don't really understand myself, for I want to do what is right, but I do not do it. Instead, I do what I hate. 16 But if I know that What I am doing is wrong, this shows that I agree that the law is good. 17 So I am not the one doing wrong; it is sin living in me that does it.

18 And I know that nothing good lives in me, that is, in my sinful nature. I want to do what is right, but I cannot. 19 I want to do what is good, but I do not. I do not want to do what is wrong, but I do it anyway. 20 But if I do what I do not want to do, I am not really the one doing wrong; it is sin living in me that does it. 21 I have discovered this principle of life—that when I want to do what is right, I inevitably do what is wrong. 22 I love God's law with all my heart. 23 But there is another power within me that is at war with my mind. This power makes me a slave to the sin that is still within me. 24 Oh, what a miserable person I am! Who will free me from this life that is dominated by sin and death? 25 Thank God! The answer is in Jesus Christ our Lord. So, you see how it is: In my mind I really want to obey God's law, but because of my sinful nature I am a slave to sin. Romans 8:2-6 2 because through Christ Jesus the law of the Spirit who gives life has set you free from the law of sin and death. 3 For what the law was powerless to do because it was weakened by the flesh, God did by sending his own Son in the likeness of sinful flesh to be a sin offering. And he condemned sin in the flesh, 4 in order that the righteous requirement of the law might be fully met in us, who do not live according to the flesh but according to the Spirit.

5 Those who live according to the flesh have their minds set on what the flesh desires; but those who live in accordance with the Spirit have their minds set on what the Spirit desires. 6 The mind governed by the flesh is death, but the mind governed by the Spirit is life and peace. 1 Thessalonians 4:4-5 3 For it is God's will that you should be holy: You must abstain from sexual immorality; 4each of you must know how to control his own body in holiness and honor, 5not in lustful passion like the Gentiles who do not know God. Galatians 5:16-This I say then, walk in the Spirit, and ye shall not fulfill the lust of the flesh.

[17] For the flesh lusts against the Spirit, and the Spirit against the flesh: and these are contrary the one to the other: so that ye cannot do the things that ye would.

[18] But if ye be led of the Spirit, ye are not under the law.

[19] Now the works of the flesh are manifest, which are these; Adultery, fornication, uncleanness, lasciviousness, [20] Idolatry, witchcraft, hatred, variance, emulations, wrath, strife, seditions, heresies, [21] Envying, murders, drunkenness, reveling, and such like: of the which I tell you before, as I have also told you in time past, that they which do such things shall not inherit the kingdom of God. [22] But the fruit of the Spirit is love, joy, peace, longsuffering, gentleness, goodness, faith, [23] Meekness, temperance: against such there is no law.

[24] And they that are Christ's have crucified the flesh with the affections and lusts.

[25] If we live in the Spirit, let us also walk in the Spirit.

[26] Let us not be desirous of vain glory, provoking one another, envying one another.

Now let us go back into the garden. In the garden man was given his command but there was someone else in the garden along with Adam and Eve. Although God came and walked with them in the garden there was another being influencing man. I am quite sure they were obey the Father in the garden but here comes the serpent: let us see what a serpent is: A serpent is a sly or treacherous person, especially one who exploits a position of trust in order to betray it. Let's talk about this serpent. The serpent just didn't walk up to the couple and started telling them they could eat from the tree. He first gained their trust. They became friendly and probably talked each day when God was not present in the garden. When people are out to destroy you because they have something against you, they do not talk much when there's a person that knows them and especially their intentions.

What did the serpent have against humankind: First, they were made in the likeness of the creator and have the very breath of God on the inside of them. They had a relationship with the Father. He visited them daily. GOD has blessed them with a beautiful paradise. A personal relationship with the creator did not sit well with Satan who had been cast out of heaven because of the iniquity that had been found in his heart.

Now Satan lurks around with his plot and plan to cause them to fall from grace. Genesis 3:1 Now the serpent was craftier than any of the wild animals the LORD God had made. He said to the woman, "Did God really say, 'You must not eat from any tree in the garden'?
Look here, the Serpent was craftier than any other animal in the garden. Crafty: clever at achieving one is aimed by indirect or deceitful methods: deceitful. This animal was clever and manipulative. We all know that the serpent is Satan. Revelation 20:2 He seized the dragon, that ancient serpent, who is the devil, or Satan, and bound him for a thousand years. **Revelation 12:9** And the great dragon was hurled down--that ancient serpent called the devil and Satan, the deceiver of the entire world. He was hurled to the earth, and his angels with him. **Revelation 20:10** And the devil who had deceived them was thrown into the lake of fire and sulfur, into which the beast and the false prophet had already been thrown. There they will be tormented day and night forever and ever.

Since we know from the scriptures that the serpent is Satan, we can realize that the reptile truly was not speaking. If the reptiles were speaking all animals were. I know you are waiting to read what about being cursed to crawl on the belly? Well before we get to that let us finish the serpent making friends with Eve and Adam.

As I stated earlier, this was not a one-time meeting, they were on speaking terms. God had already told them not to eat from this tree. You know how most were raised not to speak to strangers. This was the case here. This stranger was not good to them because he had rude habits. The main bad habit he possessed was disobedience. Now he was passing this habit off to Adam and Eve because of jealousy.

We need to understand that Satan hates us, that is, humanity. It does not make any difference if you are allowing him to use you are not. Directly to the point, Satan and all the wicked spirits hate you and me. It is time to be on the side of the one that loves you and has your best interests at heart.

Yes, Satan was cursed to crawl upon his belly, and this is why ? Simple because he is the low of the low. He was cast out to the earth to eat the dust of the earth meaning the filth of the world.

The Fall due to deception

The serpent (Satan) began to tell them that you know your loving Father will not harm you. I am quite sure he told them, "Well don't eat the fruit since you do not want to know the truth about the creator". Then he probably went on to say, "well it must be a reason why God doesn't want you to know or have knowledge". Manipulative people know how to get their point across to get you to do what they want you to do. Still man was given a direct command. Do not eat from the tree of knowledge of good and evil.

We know how it is when we hear something that we already know is too good to be true, most of us must find out if it is for real. Put a highlight here…

The knowledge of good and evil, well let us think about that. Hosea points out in 4:6 KJV [6] My people are destroyed for lack of knowledge: because thou hast rejected knowledge, I will also reject thee, that thou shalt be no priest to me: seeing thou hast forgotten the law of thy God, I will also forget thy children. Okay, we have the knowledge now but we reject what is said… Well Adam and Eve rejected the wisdom of God the "know." This was their first bite of the fruit of the tree.

Why I say this is because God already told them what would happen if they ate of the tree of knowledge. He gave them the "Word of Truth," but they rejected it. Just like so many of us today. The more we hear the word the more we go the opposite way of that word because we think we know more than God the one that created us. Now since the serpent has befriended them he put it out there and they took part of the knowledge (Satan word) over God.

Adam and Eve have now rejected God's word and took on the word of Satan. Now enters the other fruit of unrighteousness which is also disobedience.

God, as usual comes in the even of the day, calls out for Adam. Adam would always answer. Now he is afraid because he knows he has disobeyed the command of GOD.

In the garden there were 2 trees. Not actual trees, but two beings. One was Jesus and the other was Satan. Remember Jesus told his disciples Luke 10: **18** He replied, "I saw Satan fall like lightning from heaven. We all know that Jesus was always there from the beginning of time.

When man was cast out of the garden the flaming sword was placed to keep them from entering in. this when the gateway was broken between God and man. God sent his Son to allow man access back to the garden which is paradise to fellowship again with him personally.

The Two Trees in the Garden

There were two trees in the garden. One being the tree of life and the other the tree of knowledge of good and evil. **Let us see it this way.** Jesus was in the garden and so was Satan. The tree of life (Jesus) to man was not desirable to look upon. Isaiah 53:2 **2**He grew up before him like a tender shoot, and like a root out of dry ground. He had no beauty or majesty to attract us to him, nothing in his appearance that we should desire him. **3**He was despised and rejected by humankind, a man of suffering, and familiar with pain. Like one from whom people hide their faces he was despised, and we held him in low esteem. We see it so plainly here. Even in the garden he was rejected. Still today so many reject Jesus because they must give up sin for eternal life. John 14:6 - Jesus saith unto him, I am the way, the truth, and the life: no man cometh unto the Father, but by me. Proverbs 3:18 - She is a tree of life to them that lay hold upon her: and happy is every one that retained her. (Right here is reference to the Holy Spirit) if you have JESUS, you have the Father and Holy Spirit. **NIV**

Then Jesus declared, "I am the bread of life. Whoever comes to me will never go hungry, and whoever believes in me will never be thirsty. **John 8:12 I am the light of the world. Whoever follows me will not walk in darkness, but will have the light of life**

John 10:7 Truly, truly, I say to you, I am the door of the sheep (John 10:7)

John 10:11 I am the good shepherd. The good shepherd lays down his life for the sheep

John 11:25 I am the resurrection and the life. Whoever believes in me, though he dies, yet shall he live..."

John 14:6 I am the way, and the truth, and the life. No one comes to the Father except through me

John 15:5I am the vine; you are the branches. Whoever abides in me and I in him, he it is that bears much fruit, for apart from me you can do nothing

Revelation 22:14 [14]Blessed are they that do his commandments, that they may have right to **the tree of life and** may enter in through the gates into the city.

Revelation 22:1-2 [1 And] he shewed me a pure river of water of life, clear as crystal, proceeding out of the throne of God and of the Lamb. [2 In] the midst of the street of it, and on either side of the river, was there **the tree of life**, which bare twelve manners of fruits, and yielded her fruit every month: and the leaves of the tree were for the healing of the nations.

Genesis 3:22-24 [22 And] the LORD God said, Behold, the man is become as one of us, to know good and evil: and now, lest he put forth his hand, and take also of the tree of life, and eat, and live forever: [23 Therefore] the LORD God sent him forth from the garden of Eden, to till the ground from whence he was taken. [24]So he drove out the man; and he placed at the east of the garden of Eden Cherubim, and a flaming sword which turned every way, to keep the way of **the tree of life**.

JESUS the tree of life, the righteous Holy one.

Notes

Tree Two the desirable one

Tree two, Satan, he was more beautiful to look upon. Ezekiel 28:17 Your heart was proud because of your beauty; you corrupted your wisdom for the sake of your splendor. I cast you to the ground; I exposed you before kings, to feast their eyes on you. Ezekiel 28:14 You were an anointed guardian cherub. I placed you; you were on the holy mountain of God; in the midst of the stones of fire you walked. Ezekial 28: [12] Son of man, take up a lamentation upon the king of Tyrus, and say unto him, Thus saith the Lord God; Thou seals up the sum, full of wisdom, and perfect in beauty.

[13] Thou hast been in Eden the garden of God; every precious stone was thy covering, the sardius, topaz, and the diamond, the beryl, the onyx, and the jasper, the sapphire, the emerald, and the carbuncle, and gold: the workmanship of thy tabrets and of thy pipes was prepared in thee in the day that thou was created. [14] Thou art the anointed cherub that covered; and I have set thee so: thou was upon the holy mountain of God; thou hast walked up and down in the midst of the stones of fire.

[15] Thou was perfect in thy ways from the day that thou was created, till iniquity was found in thee. Satan the tree of knowledge knowing right and wrong but because sin was found in his heart, he chose the wrong path. He wants to exalt himself over his maker. Remember Jesus was there when he saw him fall like lightning from heaven when Satan was cast out of heaven.

Let me put this insert of how the Holy Spirit gave it to me a few days ago: Adam and Eve ate from the tree that they were told not to; they still receive the Knowledge of right and wrong (good and evil). They had the choice to be truthful to God when he called for Adam in the Garden. We all have this same fruit: the Knowledge of when we are doing what is not pleasing unto God our Father. Bottom line Adam and Eve were not without excuse, like so many people these days that refuse to read the Bible. God said he was writing it upon the table of our hearts.

Jeremiah 31:31-34 ESV

"Behold, the days are coming, declares the Lord, when I will make a new covenant with the house of Israel and the house of Judah, not like the covenant that I made with their fathers on the day when I took them by the hand to bring them out of the land of Egypt, my covenant that they broke, though I was their husband, declares the Lord. But this is the covenant that I will make with the house of Israel after those days, declares the Lord: I will put my law within them, and I will write it on their hearts. And I will be their God, and they shall be my people. And no longer shall each one teach his neighbor and each his brother, saying, 'Know the Lord,' for they shall all know me, from the least of them to the greatest, declares the Lord. For I will forgive their iniquity, and I will remember their sin no more

What tree are you eating from?

Let's find out which one you are eating from; Tree of Knowledge of good and evil; Which is your pattern after the fallen one Satan that one everyone calls the Devil. Well, this tree allows us to have knowledge and awareness of what we are doing on a day-to-day basis. We know when we are being disobedient to God and when we are not. Don't you know Satan knew what he was doing when he wanted to take the throne of God? Yes, he did because he also was given a choice just like you and I to obey or disobey our Creator.

Here is a list of the fruit of the tree of knowledge of good and evil by scripture. If you find yourself falling into any of these categories, it's time to repent and do what is right. 1 Corinthians 6:9–11 NIV [9] Or do you not know that wrongdoers will not inherit the kingdom of God? Do not be deceived: Neither the *sexually immoral* nor *idolaters* nor *adulterers* nor *men who have sex with men* [10] nor *thieves* nor the *greedy* nor *drunkards* nor *slanderer*s nor *swindlers* will inherit the kingdom of God. [11] And that is what some of you were. But you were washed, you were sanctified, you were justified in the name of the Lord Jesus Christ and by the Spirit of our God.

Galatians 519 The acts of the flesh are obvious: *sexual immorality*, *impurity,* and *debauchery*; 20 *idolatry* and *witchcraft*; *hatred, discord, jealousy, fits of rage, selfish ambition, dissensions, factions* 21 and *envy; drunkenness, orgies*, and the like. I warn you, as I did before, that those who live like this will not inherit the kingdom of God.:

Ephesians 5:3 But among you there must not be even a hint of *sexual immorality*, or of any kind of *impurity*, or of *greed*, because these are improper for God's holy people. 4 Nor should there be *obscenity, foolish talk,* or *coarse joking*, which are out of place, but rather thanksgiving. 5 For of this you can be sure: No *immoral, impure,* or *greedy* person—such a person is an *idolate*r—has any inheritance in the kingdom of Christ and of God. 6 Let no one deceive you with empty words, for because of such things God's wrath comes on those who are disobedient. 7 Therefore do not be partners with them. (God tells us that we are living for Him not to even partner with such people. I believe it keeps us spotless from the sins of the flesh. You know some if they stay around people that are doing these things eventually, they will convince some to do likewise. When you know you have been delivered from such things flee from it to strengthen yourself and maybe after you are strong in the faith you can help snatch someone else out.) 8 For you were once darkness, but now you are light in the Lord. Live as children of light 9 (for the fruit of the light consists in all goodness, righteousness, and truth) 10 and find out what pleases the Lord. 11 Have nothing to do with the fruitless deeds of darkness, but rather expose them. 12 It is shameful even to mention what the disobedient does in secret. 13 But everything exposed by the light becomes visible—and everything that is illuminated becomes a light.

Proverbs 6: 16 These six things doth the Lord hate: yea, seven are an abomination unto him: 17 A *proud loo*k, a *lying tongue*, and *hands that shed innocent blood,*

18 An *heart that devises wicked imaginations*, *feet that be swift in running to mischief*,

19 A *false witness that speaketh lies*, and he that *soweth discord among brethren*.

1 John 3:12 Do not be like Cain, who belonged to the evil one and *murdered* his brother. And why did he murder him? Because his own actions were evil, and his brothers were righteous.

John 8:44 Ye are of your father the devil, and the lusts of your father ye will do. He was a *murderer* from the beginning, and abode not in the truth, because there is no truth in him. When he *speaks a li*e, he speaketh of his own: for he is *a liar*, and the *father of it.*

Right here it talks about the tree. The tree is Who you want to follow and be like. Satan is the Father of lies and God is the Father of truth. Lies lead to sin and truth righteousness.

Please remember this: Revelation 21:8 But the *fearful*, and *unbelieving*, and the *abominable*, and *murderers*, and *whoremongers*, and *sorcerers*, and *idolaters*, and all *liars*, shall have their part in the lake which burneth with fire and brimstone: which is the second death. And

Revelation 22:15 For without are ***dogs***, and ***sorcerers***, and ***whoremongers***, and ***murderers***, and ***idolaters,*** and ***whosoever loveth and makes a lie.*** These listed here will not enter into the kingdom of heaven. You must choose who you want to be like, or should I say what tree you would like to eat from. Always know you can't serve two, you must make a choice.

The Tree of Life: this tree was in the Garden also. Maybe life is not important to some people. Ephesians 5: (For the fruit of the Spirit is in all goodness and righteousness and truth. 10 Proving what is acceptable unto the Lord. Galatians 5: 22 But the fruit of the Spirit is love, joy, peace, longsuffering, gentleness, goodness, faith, 23 Meekness, temperance: against such there is no law. 24 And they that are Christ's have crucified the flesh with the affections and lusts. 25 If we live in the Spirit, let us also walk in the Spirit. All of this works by Love for God is love. I made up my mind to live in the Fruit of the Spirit where there is no law. Hallelujah

In life I have found that some don't want to be loved and it's hard for them to Love. The greatest command from our Father is love God and love one another. This is where deliverance comes in. Many have been wounded and need to be healed in their hearts. Are you eating from Love? Love Romans 13:10 "Love worketh no ill to his neighbor: therefore love is the fulfilling of the law. Before I go any farther: Jesus said John 5:19 John 5:19 Jesus gave them this answer: "Very truly I tell you, the Son can do nothing by himself; he can do only what he sees his Father doing, because whatever the Father does the Son also does. If we are doing what Jesus has shown us and still teaching us through the Word and Holy Spirit, we are eating from the tree of life.

Notes

Being led by the Spirit of God

Romans 8:14 For those who are led by the Spirit of God are the children of God.

Galatian 5:18 But if you are led by the Spirit, you are not under the law. John 1:12 But as many as received him, to them gave he power to become the sons of God, even to them that believe on his name: And all those who are sons and daughters of God have the blessed hope of seeing Jesus and being like Him when he shall appear to take his children to a new heavenly home.

The Two Trees in the Garden: one was of Love/truth and righteousness and the other hatred/evil. Our actions and thoughts allow us to know which way we are going. As Joshua said to the children of Israel, Joshua 24:15 And if it seem evil unto you to serve the Lord, choose you this day whom ye will serve; whether the gods which your fathers served that were on the other side of the flood, or the gods of the Amorites, in whose land ye dwell: but as for me and my house, we will serve the Lord. I leave this with you Deuteronomy 30:19-20 NIV 19 This day I call the heavens and the earth as witnesses against you that I have set before you life and death, blessings, and curses. Now choose life, so that you and your children may live to 20 and that you may love the Lord your God, listen to his voice, and hold fast to him. For the Lord is your life, and he will give you many years in the land he swore to give to your fathers, Abraham, Isaac, and Jacob.

What is the Fruit of the Spirit

Discuss the Fruit of the Spirit according to Galatians 5:22-23 NKJV 22 But the fruit of the Spirit is love, joy, peace, longsuffering, kindness, goodness, faithfulness, **23** [a]gentleness, self-control. Against such there is no law.

Use other scriptures to clarify your discussion of each term.

____

____

____

____

____

____

____

____

____

____

John 3:16 KJV: For God so loved the world, that he gave his only begotten Son, that whosoever believeth in him should not perish, but have everlasting life.

God is Love and love covers a multitude of faults and sin. If we would just walk in Love as we were commanded the Body of Christ, the Bride would be awesome on this earth.

Word Define:

Define each word and attach several scriptures

Anger: ____

____

Sexual immorality: _______________________________

____

Impurity____

____

Greed____

____

Obsenity:____

____

Foolish talking:

____

____

Coarse joking:

____

____

Idolater:

____

____

Deceive/deceit:

____

____

Rightheousness____

____

Fruitless____

____

____

Darkness

____

____

____

Disobedient:

____

____

____

Evil:

____

____

____

How did Evil and Good begin?

____

____

____

____

Who defines what is evil and what is good?

____

____

____

How did we as human's began to know good and

evil?_____________________________________

____

____

____

Unwise:

____

____

Drunk:

Debauchery:

Dogs:

Soccery:____

____

____

____

Murderer:____

____

____

____

Falsehood/Lies/liar:____

____

____

____

Coward:____

____

____

Unbelievers;____

____

____

____

Vile:____

____

____

Magic Arts:

____

____

____

____

Servant:____

Fruit of the Spirit:

Breath of Life:

Pervert:____

____

____

____

Slander:

____

____

____

Condemnation:

____

____

____

____

Ways of Cain:

____

____

____

____

Ways of Balaam:

____

____

____

____

Sodomites:

____

____

Love:

Goodness:

Peace:

Repentance:

Forgiveness:

Remember no more:

Whoremonger:

____

____

____

____

Ten Commandments:

____

____

____

Command:

____

____

____

____

The greatest Commandment:

____

____

____

Compassion:_____________________________________

____

____

____

Adultery:

____

____

____

____

Fornication:____

____

____

____

Affections:____

____

____

____

Lusts:____

____

____

Holy Spirit:

____

____

____

Vain glory:

____

____

____

Provoking:_______________________________________

____

____

____

Envying:

____

____

____

A ***proud look:***

____

____

A *lying tongue:*

Hands that shed innocent blood:

Wicked imaginations:

*Mischief:*____

____

____

False witness that speaks lies:

____

____

____

Discord:

____

____

____

Fill in the Trees with your characteristics ******* Be honest with yourself

Tree of Life

Tree of Good and Evil

As Believers, most of us go through life as if we have it all together... Let us look at some of these fruits we are eating, are they the fruit we should be eating/producing as believers? I did not say I was the best writer, but I am obeying God. Always search for the scriptures. This Just a tool to get you thinking. I pray this will get you thinking, changing and talking as well as sharing God's Word. Use it for Bible Study as a teaching guide.

I ask myself all the time, am I producing the right fruit???? Am I eating from the right tree? According to scriptures, who am I truly serving? Now ask yourself the same questions… According to the Word of God, who are you really serving???? Are you eating from the right Tree.

Thank you for being a blessing to this ministry.

ALRM